11-13-96

D1252641

THIS CANDLEWICK BOOK BELONGS TO:

_____

_____

_____

_____

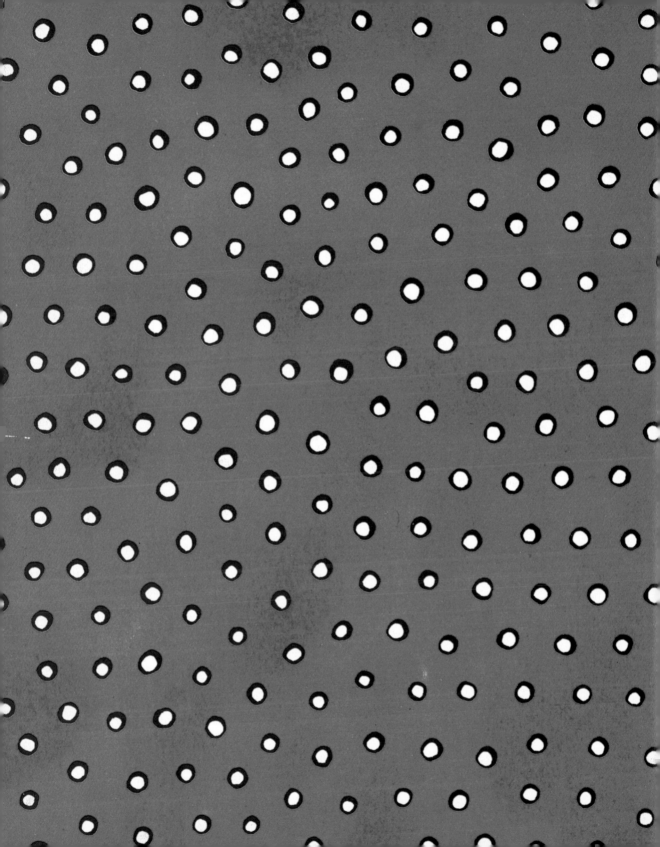

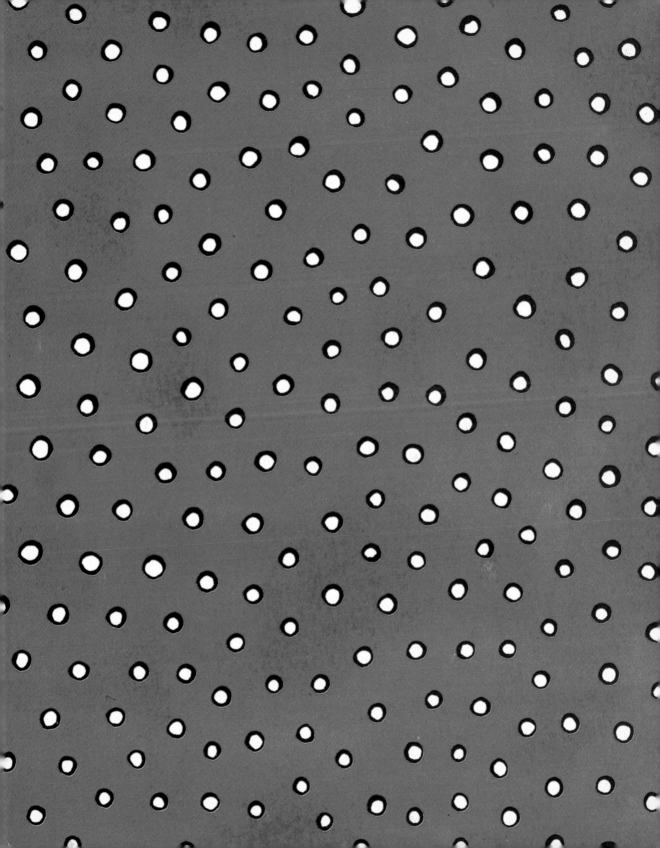

Text copyright © 1986 by Judy Hindley
Illustrations copyright © 1994 by Nick Sharratt

First U.S. edition 1996

Library of Congress Cataloging-in-Publication Data

Hindley, Judy.
Isn't it time? / Judy Hindley ; illustrated by Nick Sharratt.
Summary: Simple text matches daily activities with the
concept of telling time throughout the day.
ISBN 1-56402-458-X
1. Time—Juvenile literature. [1. Time.]
I. Sharratt, Nick, ill.   II. Title
QB209.5.H56   1996
529.7—dc20   95-363

2 4 6 8 10 9 7 5 3 1

Printed in Hong Kong

This book was typeset in Garamond Book Educational.
The pictures were done in watercolor and ink.

Candlewick Press
2067 Massachusetts Avenue
Cambridge, Massachusetts 02140

Isn't It Time?

Judy Hindley

illustrated by

Nick Sharratt

CANDLEWICK PRESS
CAMBRIDGE, MASSACHUSETTS

Ticktock, ticktock, ticktock,

bleeep!

Wake up! Wake up!

It's seven o'clock in the morning!

Isn't it time you were up and about?

Quick, wake up!

Get up!

Get out!

Look at the sky! Look at the sun!

Look at all of us on the run!

It's time to wake up at our house!

Eight o'clock, eight o'clock . . .

Isn't it time to go?

Around the house,

around the block,

everyone knows it's eight o'clock!

They're eating their toast

and cleaning their shoes,

and washing and dressing,

and reading the news.

It's time to be ready to go!

Nine o'clock, nine o'clock . . .

Isn't it time for school?

Hang up your coat!

Sit in your chair!

You know we can't start

until everyone's here,

and it's time for the bell to go.

Brrring!

It's time for our school to start!

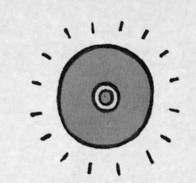

Ten o'clock, ten o'clock . . .

Isn't it time for milk?

Look at your hands!

Look at your face!

Wash out your brushes!

Clean up the place!

We're thirsty.

It's time for some milk!

Eleven o'clock, eleven o'clock . . .

Isn't it time to go out?

Isn't it time to sing and shout,

and jump and fight and rush about?

Everyone else wants to play.

Hey!

It's time to go out and play!

Twelve o'clock, twelve o'clock . . .

Aren't you a little bit hungry yet?

There's salad and sandwiches

and potato chips too—

but soon there'll be nothing at all for you.

Hurry!

It's time to eat!

One o'clock, one o'clock . . .

Isn't it time for a rest?

Isn't it time to sit quietly down

with your feet on the floor

and your chair on the floor

and your head on your hands

on your desk?

Sshhh!

It's time for the story to start!

Two o'clock, two o'clock . . .

Isn't it time for a walk?

Outside in the sun,

there's a world going on,

creeping and hopping

and flying and hiding,

down in the puddles,

up in the trees,

and under the stones on the lawn.

Come on!

It's time for our nature walk!

What time is it? Look at the clock.

Three o'clock!

Run!

Time to go home

and tidy up.

What a long day it's been!

We had to get up at seven o'clock,

and be ready to go at eight o'clock,

and start our lessons at nine o'clock,

and have our milk at ten o'clock,

and go out to play at eleven o'clock,

and eat our lunch at twelve o'clock,

and have our story at one o'clock,

and go for our walk at two o'clock,

and get very busy at three o'clock,

because . . . because at four o'clock—

knock, knock, knock, knock . . .

It's time for the party to start!

Five o'clock, five o'clock . . .

Isn't it time for the games to stop?

Isn't it time for the prizes now?

Isn't it time for the sweets?

Isn't it time for the birthday cake?

Isn't it time to eat?

Six o'clock, six o'clock . . .

Isn't it time for the presents?

Now!

Open them up.

What's in the box?

Ticktock . . .

Wow!

So isn't it time to tell the time?

Look at it.

What does it say?

Seven o'clock, seven o'clock,

the end of a wonderful day.

Sleep well, sleep tight,

it's seven o'clock, seven o'clock,

seven o'clock

at night.

Ticktock,

ticktock,

tick-tick-tick-tick-tick . . .

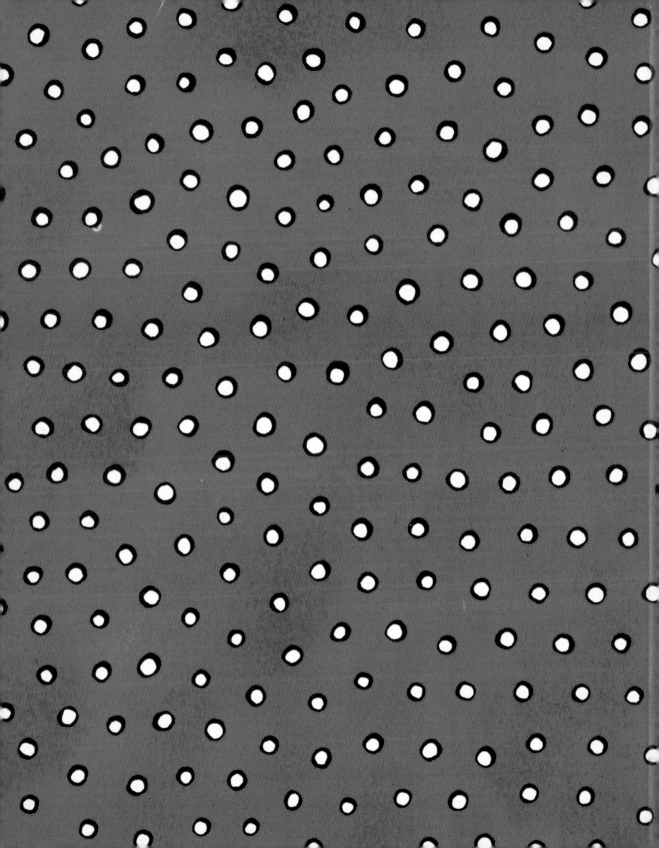

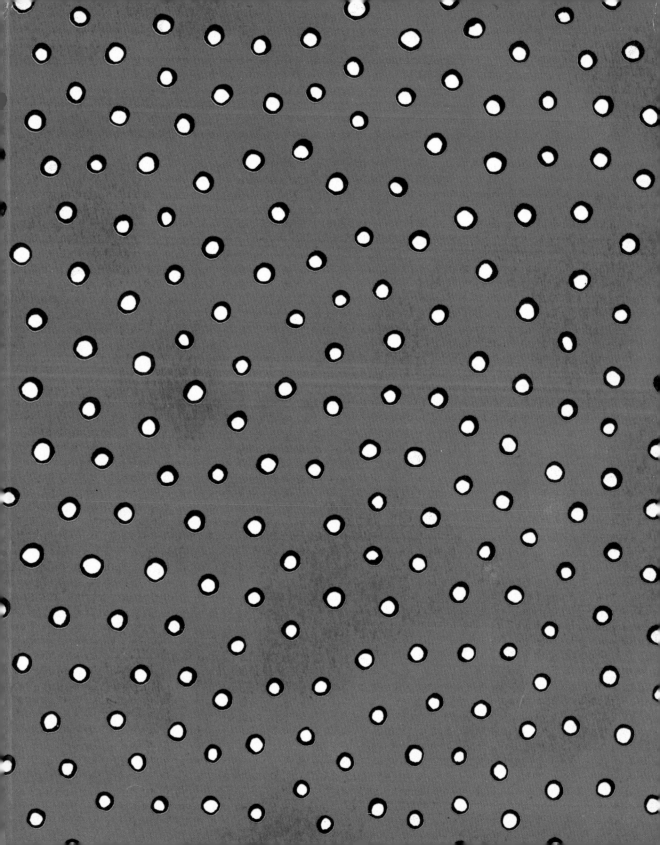

JUDY HINDLEY, a graduate of the University of Chicago, has written more than thirty books for children, including *A Piece of String Is a Wonderful Thing* and *The Wheeling and Whirling-Around Book*, both Candlewick Read and Wonder books, as well as *Into the Jungle*. She says this book is "meant to be read aloud; to be shared by a child and an adult. Children learn best when they're having fun *with* someone."

NICK SHARRATT loves striking patterns and bold colors, as is evident in his vibrant books *Rocket Countdown*, *My Mom and Dad Make Me Laugh*, *Monday Run-Day*, *The Green Queen*, *Snazzy Aunties*, and *Mrs. Pirate*. He comments that illustrating Judy Hindley's books was "really enjoyable; I felt completely in tune with Judy's poetry."